I0136532

Frank Sewall

The new Ethics

An Essay on the Moral Law of Use

Frank Sewall

The new Ethics
An Essay on the Moral Law of Use

ISBN/EAN: 9783337232573

Printed in Europe, USA, Canada, Australia, Japan

Cover: Foto ©Suzi / pixelio.de

More available books at **www.hansebooks.com**

THE NEW ETHICS

AN ESSAY ON

THE MORAL LAW OF USE

BY

FRANK SEWALL

———

NEW YORK

G. P. PUTNAM'S SONS

27 & 29 WEST 23D STREET

1881

Press of
G. P. Putnam's Sons
New York

CONTENTS.

THE NEW ETHICS.

CHAPTER I

THE obscurity attaching to the subject of ethics as a science and to ethical education as a practical achievement, is owing, doubtless, to the vagueness of the notions entertained as to what man's moral nature is, if indeed there be any such thing, and then as to what can be done with it by that process which we term educational. Education as applied to the bodily or intellectual faculties is an intelligible term. Let us accept the definition of it which seems most commonly approved, that it is, namely, the awakening and calling into exercise of the faculties that are in man and their adaptation to his surroundings. What, in the case of ethics, is the moral faculty, and is there a moral surrounding to which it is, by education, to be harmoniously fitted? It is on these questions that the author hopes in the following pages to throw some light.

Difficulty in defining the moral nature.
It is not so strange as might at first appear, that while the physical training and the intellectual education of man have been for so long a time reduced to a science and to practical methods, the training of the moral part of our being is still a thing of doubt and guesses and only half-admitted conclusions. When we reflect on the nature of the subject itself as being distinctly unintellectual, as belonging rather to the substantive than to the formative part of our nature, as being a thing of feeling and not of definite, formulated thought, we can partially comprehend how it is that while all men feel conscious of a moral nature, of moral impulses from within, of moral influences from without,

Will confounded with intellect.
and of moral ends to be attained, still ·the moment we begin with our definitions and rules the matter itself slips mysteriously from our grasp, and we find that we are formulating

after all a science of dialectics, a science of thought and of reasoning, and not that of the will and its nature at all. We fall again into the old snare into which Socrates fell in declaring that virtue is a knowledge, and that knowing the right would be practically equivalent to doing the right. The human mind cannot thus legislate itself into virtue individually, any more than it can collectively or in the form of the State. It would seem that the first step of essential progress in the definitions of ethics is to be found in Aristotle's distinguishing between the will as the affectional part of the human mind and the intellect as the instrument of thought. With this grand dual division of man's nature acknowledged, and in the light which a more recent and profound spiritual science has thrown upon it, we are enabled to proceed upon comparatively solid and certain ground in our definitions and analysis of ethics as a whole. Man is before us as a being of twofold nature, a being of feeling and of thought, of

Error of Socrates.

Aristotle: first step in true definition.

Analysis of the mind: its twofold nature.

emotion and of reflection, of will and of intellect.

Will and
intellect.   A deeper analysis still of the human mind
reveals the substance or primary force of the
human life itself to be the emotions, the desires, the love which resides in and makes up
the will of man, and that the thoughts and the
ideas which occupy the other or intellectual
half of the mind are but the forms, the conscious representations of the contents of the
will.   Thus affection and thought are corre-
lated like every substance with its own form.
They are one, and yet not the same ; they are
one, but distinctly one ; they can be thought of
Intellect
gives form apart, yet cannot exist apart.   To illustrate :
to emotions
of the will. an emotion of the will is doubtless felt as such
in the will, but it has to go to the intellect to
acquire a form, a definite shape or determination.   We cannot be said to know our desires,
to define them, much less to carry them into
execution, until the desire has clothed itself
with a judgment or a form of thought from

the intellect. Thus, while our emotions or feelings are shapeless and ineffectual without the
idea and the judgment of the intellect to serve
them as instruments of action, so on the other
hand the judgment and reasoning of the intel
lect are soulless and lifeless when influenced
with no purpose or motive from the will.
Thoughts which are not the clothing of the af- Thoughts without substance.
fections are but ghosts of thoughts, and if ut-
tered or written, soon show their emptiness
and unreality.

The intellect, therefore, is the depository of
those forms in which as ideas or judgments the
will comes to a knowledge of itself, or presents
itself to the intelligence of others. So inti-
mate is the union of the emotional and the intellectual parts, as before intimated, that philosophers from Socrates down have been con-
stantly liable to the mistake of confounding the Error of the ancients.
two, and treating of the will or the affectional
part of man as capable of a kind of intellectual
training, or as subject to a kind of intellectual

analysis; and this mistake has partly arisen from the difficulty naturally adhering to the consideration of any substance in itself or apart from the forms in which it presents itself to thought and reflection.

Education of the intellect.
The education of the intellect, itself the form of the mind, and at once the recipient of forms in impressions of the senses and the producer of forms in its own imagination, has been a comparatively simple science from the beginning. Whether we guide the child's mind by objective demonstrations, or from the contemplation of one form outwardly presented to that of another, or conduct the maturer student through the imaginary forms of the higher mathematics, or through the subtle conclusions of logic as applied to abstract questions of society and religion ; in either case we have that to deal with the very being of which is law and uniformity, and which, therefore, is capable of rapidly developing into a genuine science. Hence it is that intellectual education has been

at all times far in advance of that of the moral
nature. Not only in the classic but in modern
nations we have not unfrequently been struck
by a strange coincidence of a period of brilliant
intellectual activity with that of great moral
stagnation and corruption, all of which goes to
show that the intellect is a comparatively external part of man, near the surface, capable as
well of disguising as of truly revealing the real
man within, and susceptible of a training from
without by means entirely discordant, it may
be, to the impulses of the will within.

Not coincident with moral culture.

Intellect the external and artificial man.

IF we turn now to the will itself, to this man
of desire, of emotion, of pure feeling, and try to
contemplate him, first, as a subject of education,
and, secondly, as an agent striving to achieve an
end, or better still, as the end, the impulse and
aim itself, which animates all the intellectual
and physical life below itself; here we shall enter the real domain of ethics and ethical education.

CHAPTER II.

Will the internal and real man.

We will not, indeed, try to think of the will

or feeling as entirely formless, that is, entirely
independent of those ideal vessels or shapes
furnished by the intellect, but we will try to
contemplate pure feeling in itself as far as possible, knowing that the moment we define it as
a feeling of something, a desire of something, it
truly becomes a thought and thus an intellectual act as well as a feeling.   Indeed, pure emotion, or emotion in general, which is not a being
moved mentally from or to some particular object, we may safely say does not exist.   Consciousness does not exist except as consciousness of some state, or its modification.   But
while this is quite true, it is also true that there
are certain abstractions of state or of forms, or
we may perhaps better say universals of states
of consciousness, which are, seemingly, more
truly things of feeling than of intellect, and
these are the sensations of pleasure and pain, or,
in moral terms, the judgments of the good and
the bad.

The will or the affectional nature of man does

The
universal
feeling;
pleasure
and pain.

seem indeed capable of forming immediate judgments of good and of bad, of the pleasant and the unpleasant, without the intervention of any conclusions or even idea of the intellect. We may feel pleasure and feel pain, not, it is true, to the exclusion from the mind of some object of the thoughts at the same time as perhaps the occasion of the feeling, but still, as a sensation or experience by itself, an acting distinctly of the will or of that part of one which feels and does not think.

Now, this part of man which feels is, as I have said, that which is to be considered in moral culture. To affect it for good or bad is to affect the foundation of our intelligent and responsible life. Behind the man that acts, that speaks, that reasons, that thinks, that desires even, is the man that feels, that loves. The life of man itself is his love.

The feelings, the subject of moral culture.

It will now be apparent how admirable was the classification which Kant and other German psychologists have borrowed from the

Ethics a branch of æsthetics.

Greek philosophers, by which ethics was treated of as a department of æsthetics. For what is æsthetics but the science of taste? Is it not the science of our faculty of perceiving pleasure and pain through the sensations contemplated in their several grades?

I.
Æsthetics
on the
physical
plane, or
*sensuous
taste.*

I. Thus in the lowest plane æsthetics deals with the feelings as mere physical or bodily touch ; which grade of taste embraces the æsthetic judgments of all immediate sensations of the body, not only of taste so-called, and smell, and touch, as affording pleasure and pain, but also the affection of the eye in beautiful form and color, or of the ear in beautiful sounds or harmonies.

II.
Æsthetics
on the
intellectual
plane, or
*mental
taste.*

II. On the second or intellectual plane the æsthetic judgments embrace the sensations of the pleasant and the unpleasant in ideas and thoughts formed by the mind of another, more especially as subject to the laws of intellectual beauty or harmony and completeness.

III. In the moral plane the æsthetic judg-

ments embrace the sensations of pleasure and
pain, or of the good and bad in those things
that relate to conduct, to the motives of men,
to the loves that inspire them, the desires that
impel them, the pleasures that allure them, the
evils that repel them. Thus, elevate the sense
of touch or of feeling from the body to the in-
ner man, the will itself as the inmost of a man's
life and conduct, and we have æsthetics in its
moral degree, or in that degree which has been
more generally denominated that of ethics, or
the laws which control our judgments of the
good and the bad.

According to this classification, ethics is re-
ducible to a science of taste, nay of touch ; it
treats of the will of man as subject to sensations of pleasure and of pain from moral objects
presented to it, as capable of contact with outward impressions of a moral nature, and as
being stimulated by these impressions to either
one or another course of conduct. The will of
man has its finer sense of touch, by which it

III. Æsthetics on the moral plane, or *ethics*.

Ethics is the moral taste.

comes in contact with a universe about itself, yet like unto itself, just as in the lower plane, the body, with its sensations, comes in contact with a material universe of agreeable or disagreeable objects.

The subject of ethical education.

Such, then, is the will and moral nature of man as a subject of education.

CHAPTER III.

THE question which next arises is, into what is the will to be educated? What is the object or aim in moral or ethical education?

The object in view in ethical education: analogy with intellectual and physical education.

In answering this question we shall be helped by first observing the analogous cases of physical and intellectual culture. From these more familiar and easily accessible processes, we may conclude with greater certainty regarding the somewhat obscure theme, the education of the moral nature.

What, then, is the aim of physical education? What is a healthy development of the body? What was the grand aim of the gymnastics of the Greeks? Was it not an adaptation of the body in all its parts, its functions and motions,

The body to be in harmony with nature.

to the law of nature as bearing upon the physical good of man? It was a training of the body into a harmony with the physical universe, into such a harmony that the waves of sound, and of light, and of the magnetic aura of the earth's atmosphere, should be transmitted in beautifully harmonious undulations of more subtle media through all the tissues and fibres of the body, producing there exhilaration, concord, joy, and recreation. On the other hand, the will and thought should find a perfect and ready and mighty instrument in the body for transmitting its emotion and desires in the forms of effectual act and profitable labor in the field of matter, so that, not only should the body perfectly reflect and respond to objective nature, but also nature should be brought to perfect obedience to human force and mind through the exercise of the bodily powers.

To take now the next step, do we not find in intellectual education the aim to be an analo- The intellect to be in harmony with truth.

gous one? We have here the mind of man, considered intellectually, to be developed into harmony with the universal laws of truth, so that the truth shall readily enter it and find a welcome in a quick perception ; so that in creating new images and forming new conclusions in inductive reasoning, the mind shall be secure from fallacies, and reason in strict accordance with the internal *logos* or reason of the universe. A trained intellect is not one crowded with crude knowledge, but one capable of clear analytical thought, secure against delusions, whether from sense or from sophistries or logical snares, one that can look through effects to causes, and through causes to ends, and thus see the laws of order upon which not only the universe is constructed and exists, but without which there could be no determination of the true or false.

A trained intellect is one capable of detecting the truth or falsity of a thing as determined by a universal law appertaining to that thing. Of course the existence of this universal law is pre-supposed in every judgment of the intellect as to the true or false. In other words, there are no particular truths if there is no universal truth or universally true law.

We come now to the moral plane of the mind, and from analogy may we not assert that the object of education is to adapt this part of man's nature to the moral laws of the universe about him, and to render man so evenly, symmetrically, and wholly developed a moral instrument, one so delicately tuned, so to speak, as to its least vibrating fibre, that it shall respond harmoniously to the pulsations of the moral atmosphere without ; that it shall be susceptible of all the finer and purer emotions of moral influence, and be able to send out from itself again strong vibrating currents of purpose, feeling, and motion, which shall fall readily into the great moral currents without, and be developing wider and wider spheres of good and delight to eternity? In other words, is not every

[Margin note: The object of moral education is to adapt man to the moral law of the universe.]

man morally as to his emotions and desires the centre of a universe in which action and reaction is forever going on according to fixed laws, just as he is, by universal consent, the centre of a similar physical and intellectual world?

CHAPTER IV.

Divided opinions. Is there an objective moral law of the universe?

At this point, I am well aware, and perhaps here first in the progress of our discussion, opinion divides, and whichever position is taken, whether for or against an objective moral law, and an objective moral law-giver, for one implies the other, it will be liable to dispute from those holding opposite views. But it will be seen, I think, that no discussion of ethics as a practical matter, least of all as a matter of education, is possible without one or the other of these positions being definitely taken. For if education is the development of the subject into harmony with its environment, then in moral education we presuppose a moral environment, and to arrive at a true notion of what this actually is, is probably the most important ethical problem before the world to-day.

Without endeavoring, therefore, to conceive what the basis of an ethical education might be with those who deny the existence of any such moral environment of man, or objective moral law, any universal distinctions of right and wrong, or good and evil in the universe, I shall proceed to carry out our analogy in de- A universal fining ethical education as a development of assumed. the emotional nature of man into harmony with the universal laws of good and evil in the world around him ; such a development that the really good will be felt by him as good in giving him pleasure, and the really bad will be felt by him as bad in giving him pain.   As by the well-trained intellect a fallacy in an argu- ment or a fault in a literary work is felt as actu- ally harsh or grating to the refined intellectual sense, so to the correctly trained moral nature, an exhibition of bad behavior, a suggestion of evil conduct, will produce a real sensation of pain or disgust and revulsion.   Such a relation of man's moral sense to the moral world about him, I hold to be a true and actual one, and upon this as a real substantial basis afforded in the very nature of things, a practical system of ethical training is conceivable.

The education implies two factors—a subject to be trained, and a law or standard by which to train it. This training presupposes, as I have already said, two factors : first, a sense to be appealed to ; and, second, a law or a standard which is absolute and fixed, by which all sensations are adjudged as harmonious or as discordant with the moral order and harmony of the universe, and thus as really delightful or undelightful to the moral sense.

The sense itself is the will of man in its susceptibility to moral emotions, or as capable of being made happy or sad by impressions from moral objects ; thus, by exhibitions of emotion in others, by direct expressions of feeling, by persuasions, by threats, by sympathy with others' states of feeling, this sense can be cultivated to a finer and finer degree of sensibility, so that nothing going on without shall fail to convey its moral impress together with the physi.

cal sensation and its intellectual image. The
sense of the good and the bad will be quite as
spontaneous in its action as the sense of the
straight or crooked, or of the odd and even num-
bers, or of the beauty or the ugliness of a figure,
or the truth or the untruth of a proposition.

Such, we conceive, is the sense which may What is the
be educated and the capacity of its education. moral law?
The equally important inquiry is : What shall
we call this universal law of good and bad
which this sense is to be taught to know, and
by which it is to form its judgments, and control its own indulgences, and determine its own
purposes and desires?

A sane man will not spend time in thinking
out some fanciful theory for the mere delight of
the thinking, when he learns that there is a fallacy lurking in one of his premises.

So a morally sane person will not allow himself to look for pleasure in some emotion or desire
which he knows is discordant with the laws of
universal good and universal happiness. Even

a transient delight will be sacrificed sooner than
to lose a permanent and substantial good, and
those delights which will interfere with or destroy
the soul's capacity to unite itself with the universal moral harmony will come to be regarded
as not delights, but as disorderly emotions, to be
dreaded and shunned.

Laws are forms of substances and their operations. What, then, is this universal law of good
which prevails in the universe of mind, of hu-
man motive and action, just as surely and invariably as the laws of gravitation prevail in the
universe of matter? And, since all laws are
but forms of a substance, and the law of gravitation but the form in which a force or substance

What is the universal force? operates, what, therefore, is the substance or
force of good, which operates throughout the
universe of men's minds, causing happiness and
health in those which are in harmony with itself, and misery and disease in those who act
in conflict with it.

Matthew Arnold's definition—subjective only. Matthew Arnold has offered us a definition
of this universal moral force, in what he calls the

"enthusiasm which makes for righteousness."
But this is rather a subjective than an objective
element, something that impels a man from within rather than that which, within and without,
controls the whole universe of mind and matter
in such a wonderful harmony that by yielding
to it a man finds himself at one with the very law,
purpose, and end of the Divine Creator himself,
and accordingly restored to a state of orderly
relation, not with man alone, but with the
physical universe, and with all supernatural and
spiritual forms as well.

The force and law we have in view is some- *The true law is both objective and subjective —it is:—*
thing to which man must conform himself at
the same time that he becomes inwardly an
agent of it.

WE shall call this law by a new name—not, in- CHAPTER V. *The law of use.*
deed, new in every sense, but new in the sense
here intended. We shall call it the *law of use*,
and we will at once distinguish the sense in
which we employ the word.

This law of use, which is, we may say, the

divine end of the universe put into effect, is the
law of service ; but the law of mutual service,
Illustrated in creation. not the service of self.   Upon this law we hold
the universe was constructed from its first ema-
nation in spheres of divine energy and light and
heat out of the Creator himself to the elementary
plane of nature.   The same law governs the
three realms of nature, mineral, vegetable, and
animal, in their upward climbing to man, the
highest type of creation, and from whose rational and voluntary nature there is the conscious
aspiration and return again to Deity.

The Deity proceeding and returning.   Thus is completed the divine and never-ceas-
ing current of infinite *love* as a first end or
prime mover, operating by infinite *wisdom*, as
by the spiritual means or instrumental cause, *to*
the production of infinite *uses* as effects in the
plane of nature and of humanity.   Thus the
The divine origin of use. very essential nature of Deity is the giving of
itself for another, or the creating of a universe
which may be an object of love to a being
whose essence it is to love ; a universe not cre-

ated from nothing but from the eternal substance of Deity itself, and yet in such a way that it may be ever distinct from Deity, just as every action is the effect of a desire and thought and is yet distinct from these, or as an artist's crea- tion is from him and of him as to its whole for- mative principle and being and is yet not him- self, nor does its distinct existence imply a pro- portional lessening of his own substance.

Creation is the giving of self to others.

So God is conceived of as himself existing only to serve, and in finding the fullest and divinest satisfaction in the service of others than himself. God is the great creator and never- resting performer of uses. The whole universe is a great work of uses, and not the smallest atom exists in its material depths, nor the purest angel in its celestial spheres, which is not actuated wholly by this one universal divine law of life, and order, and happines, *the mutual service of things.*

God exists only to serve !

The universe exhibits everywhere this law of mutual service

Says Swedenborg, in his work on *The Divine Love and Wisdom*, No. 327 : "All things created

"by the Lord are uses; and they are uses in
"the order, degree, and respect in which they
"have relation to man and by man to the Lord
"their Creator."*

The *conatus* of use in nature.

There is a *conatus*, a struggling and yearning
of Nature from her inmost and subtlest particles
to be of use to something above herself. The
sun's heat and light, combining with the ele-
ments of the soil, strive to help the seed to ger-
minate ; the plants crowd and push in the dark
ground until they can shoot joyfully upward,
and offer their whole being as nourishment,
protection, or refreshment to either the bodily
or affectional life of the animal kingdom. The
lower animals serve the higher; all the lower
kingdoms serve man, and man serves God in a
true sense only by serving his fellow-man.
This sublime law of use, which, like all things of
divine completeness and majesty, is at once a
type of simplicity and humility, found indeed its
highest embodiment in Him who proved His
own Divinity among men, not by receiving the

* See Note 1.

homage of inferior creatures, but by *doing the works of God*, and who, as if to write forever in the mind of humanity the noblest of all legends as betokening the true knight-errantry to which all mankind is by nature called and consecrated, uttered once, in the hearing of men, these words: " I am among you as one that serves."

God the type of perfect service.

THIS law of use, or mutual service, which I have called the moral law of the universe, is readily distinguished from those other motives which have been made fundamental in the various ethical and religious systems of past times. It is essentially different from the theory which declares the end of life and man's existence to be the glory of God in the sense of the selfish delight of an arbitrary and powerful ruler in experiencing the abject subjugation and servitude of inferior creatures. The end of man is, indeed, the glory of God, but God's glory has no higher or nobler manifestation than in the uses of the universe in the mutual service of creature to creature. It is in the interchange of human

CHAPTER VI.
The law of use *distinguished:*

I. From the doctrine of the " glory of God" as the end of life.

What is the true glory of God and the kingdom of heaven?

"The
kingdom of
heaven
a kingdom
of *uses*." uses that men find at once the highest humanity
and most intense happiness. "The kingdom of
"heaven," says Swedenborg again, "is a king-
"dom of uses," and no man shall become the
happy subject of this kingdom who has not become that which he was born to become, a form
or an agency of use. To serve, not to be served,
is the highest end of man ; and the greatest
man is the man who in his gifts and actions,
whether intellectual or moral, is the means of
the greatest amount of use to his fellow-men.

Distinguished
from those
of the
Utilitarian
and
the Pietist. Compared again with the doctrine of the
Utilitarians,* or of those who would make self-
interest, even to self-love, the foundation of all
moral and social stability, and reduce the useful
to only that which is useful to self more or less
directly, the law of use which we are assert-
ing, is seen to be quite different. This makes
Service
not of *self*
but
of others. always the neighbor and not self the object
of the endeavor or the service, and regards
one's own advantage, or wealth, health, power,
and faculties, as only greater means to the

* See Note II.

NOTES.

real end in view, the good to be accomplished for others. This use, or "the good," becomes neither the dead and inert matter of mere physical gratification or bodily well-being on the one hand, as with the more materialistic Utilitarian, nor, on the other hand, the mere abstract goodness of the pietist or the theist, to whom God is a being so entirely without body, parts, and passions, as to be essentially nothing. It is, on the contrary, the most concrete and intelligible thing of every-day experience. Good is nothing except the putting into effect of a desire of use, and cannot exist abstracted from a personal will and intelligence. God is good because He is the creator and eternal *doer of useful things.* All good works are uses, and all uses done for another than a merely selfish end are genuinely, nay, divinely good. In this most true sense, God, indeed, contemplates still in the process of the never-ending days of creation, the result of each day's work which He has made, and behold it is very good.

Goodness no abstraction.

"Good works" are uses.

"Doing good" and "being good."

The phrase "to do good," and "to be "good," is lifted from the drear inanity of aimless sentiment into the noble plane of action. Goodness, as held up to a child's mind as a motive of life, means no longer a mere feeble yielding to another's violence and dying at an early age. It means the being and doing of service to one's fellow-being. It is most true that in this sense a law of good pervades all inanimate nature.

Nature "does good" but instinctively, not rationally nor morally.

Not a mineral or plant but what obeys it, and obeys it in the sense of its being the operation of personal will and intelligence ; but in this case, that which we call inanimate, is only so in being more absolutely animated from God only, than is the case with the free moral animation of man. The question which is often asked, of

The uses of nature not all material or physical.

what use is all the loveliness and elegance of form and color lavished upon flower and plumage, and tinting even the evanescent clouds, may be answered best in the simple words : the use of giving delight to the affections of living creatures, and of making man a fuller recipient of

the love of his Maker, and thus the more grate-
ful dispenser of it to others. God ministers
through the useful contrivances of nature not
to man's stomach alone, but to his affections
and his thoughts; and all the glories of creation
are provided to be of use to that life of man's
will and love which is more than meat, and that
body of his immortal reason and thought which
is more than raiment.

Finally, as compared with the ethics of Plato,
this law of use is far more a doing than a
knowing ; as compared with the Stoic's virtue
of duty and a passionless indifference to pleasure or pain, it indeed has a pleasure in view,
but a pleasure that is experienced only in regarding the good of others as first end, and is
lost when this order is inverted and the good
of others is made subservient to one's own
pleasure. As compared with the ascetic vir-
tues of the monastic orders, whether of the
Christian or of other religions, the law of use
subordinates all rules, all practices, whether of

III.
Distinguished
from ethics
of Plato.

IV.
From the
Stoics.

V.
From the
Ascetics.

prayer or work, whether fasting and morti-
fication, or bodily and mental recreation by
means of healthy sports, games, and feastings,
to the one most catholic, general, benefi-
cent, and divine rule :—" That is good which is
That is
good which
serves. " in the order óf the uses of God's universe ;
" that is good which helps man in his own sta-
" tion to be a larger, stronger, and more perfect
" agent of good, whether spiritual or rational or
" physical, to his fellow-creatures.   He best
" serves God who serves his fellow-man."

It is not necessary to dwell longer in defining use as the universal ethics of creation ; it
will be proper here to add, in conclusion, a few
reflections on the ethical education as based
upon the recognition of this law ; and first as
Moral
culture to
be
distinguished
from
intellectual. to the distinction necessary to observe between
moral and intellectual culture.   There can be
no ethics, properly speaking, without dialectics,
any more than there can be an affection as a
subject of reflection without the thought in
which that affection forms itself in the intel-

lect. Moral culture without some intellectual culture is impossible. The very form of good is the right ; and the right is the intellectual apprehension of the good. The good is the substance of the law ; the right is the form which the law gives it. The will by its higher æsthetics is aware of the distinction between the good and the evil as truly as the body feels its sensations of pleasure and pain. But man cannot act morally except he acts in freedom and from reason. It is by intelligent or self-conscious reason that man approves or disapproves of acts, and so makes himself morally responsible for them. A brute would be virtuous if its orderly instinctive life, instead of being guided immediately by a divine intelligence, were guided by the conclusions of its own reason and the determinations of its own free choice. Man is thus guided, and is therefore a responsible moral agent. But while thus the intellect is so necessary to the moral agency of the will, and a man must know what

The right or the law is the *form* of *good.*

How man differs from the brute.

the right is before he can do what is good in
preference to what is bad, we must be careful
not to reverse the case, and hold that the mere
intellectual power of distinguishing the right
from the wrong is itself moral culture. The
affection, the desire, the sense of use and its

The love needs culture— not the thought only. love must itself be cultivated by example,
stimulus, and exercise, and from the earliest
beginning of mental impressions.

The power of moral culture illustrated. The power of such a moral aim we have
seen illustrated in the patriotism of the Spartan
state especially, narrow and imperfect as was
its conception of the law of human use. The
Spartan lived for an end, the power of the
state over the subject, and the military pre-
dominance of Sparta over the neighboring
tribes and states. The mothers taught this,
the schools reëchoed it, the state exhibited it;
life was comparatively of little worth so far as
it did not contribute to this common end. A
similar, but spasmodic and temporary enthusiasm has seized other nations at other times, as

that of the Crusades and Knight-errantry in
the Middle Ages, and that of the great national
uprisings of England, France, and our own
country for the attainment of popular rights
or the preserving of national integrity. These
motives are not things of intellectual culture ;
they come from a contact of wills, from great
currents of feeling, permeating the minds of
society and stirring up the depths of emotion
or the sources of action.

But how poor and insufficient is the moral
impulse and education which animated Greece _{Insufficiency of Greek morals.}
in her noblest days, because founded on a mis-
taken law, is abundantly shown in the career of
her greatest generals, men like Themistocles
and Pausanias, who made the glory of their
states only the bridge of their own personal
ambition, and who died in disgrace as traitors
to the powers their valor had served. The
same ruinous principle of self-love as underly-
ing public service is equally exhibited in the
careers of Cicero and Cato of Rome, and, among

modern leaders, in Napoleon Bonaparte. However great the literary and military legacy of
these men, how poor is their contribution to the
moral forces of society as compared with that of
the humblest Christian martyr of whatever sect
or clime, who, for the love of God and his fellow-
men, has held dearer than life his adherence to
the truth as the revealed law of the eternal
goodness! Compare, too, on a still larger scale,
the periods of the greatest intellectual with that
of the greatest moral eminence of nations.
How often do we find the golden age of letters,
as that of Greece, of Rome, or of our own England, to be the age of a more than ordinarily
corrupt and dissolute social and public life.

CHAPTER
VII.

The
danger
threatening
our
educational
progress.

PERHAPS there is no greater danger threatening the educational progress of our own time
and our own land than this over-estimate of
mere intellectual culture and the confounding
of it with moral progress. If history teaches us
anything like a general law, it is that the cultiva-
tion of the head and of the heart do not necessa-

rily go together, and that of the two a sound moral training of a people is of greater importance to real human happiness and welfare than brilliant intellectual culture. The great argument held out nowadays for the promotion of education, and especially of free schools, is that intelligence prevents or reduces crime. I think that before long the American people will begin to question this statement, or, at least, to ask whether or not it must be modified to include a restrictive phrase that moral and not alone intellectual culture is necessary to protect society from crime. If statistics are appealed to, while it may appear that the universal stimulus given to the intellect of our young men and women has tended in our more advanced communities to the reduction of the grosser and more outwardly offensive forms of vice and immorality, it is not so evident that at the heart of society, at its very core and kernel in the secret plane of the moral consciousness where dwells all that is most sacred and pure and noble in humanity,

Does our present free-school system diminish crime?

Does intellectual culture abolish or only conceal vice?

there is not growing a sore of immorality which will sooner or later make a whited sepulchre of all this mere outside polish of mind.

Indeed, it may be a question whether the effect of mere increased intelligence, without accompanying moral principle, may not be either to invent new forms of dishonesty and vicious practice, or to cover up and ingeniously shield from penalty those crimes which with the more ignorant are not more prevalent, but are only not so cunningly and successfully concealed. I think that at least a large proportion of the excess of criminality attaching to the uneducated classes in statistical reports may be attributed, not to a real excess of crime, but to a lack of intelligent concealment; but even reading the figures as they are, the moral elevation produced by intellectual culture is by no means everywhere apparent.

Statistics show America and Massachusetts especially to have a high percentage of educated population.

From the last census of the United States, it would, indeed, appear that for one crime committed by an educated person there are ten committed (and detected) by an illiterate person. In France, from 1867 to 1869, one half of the inhabitants could neither read nor write, and this one half, or the illiterate half of the population, furnishes eighty-seven per cent. of the detected and convicted criminals; and in Massachusetts, where only seven in a hundred cannot read and write, eighty per cent. of the crimes committed (and detected) are committed by this small minority. This would appear certainly, at first glance, abundantly to vindicate the claim of education as being the effectual preventive of crime.

United States, France, Massachusetts.

But how far these figures indicate the moral influence of education itself, in not merely concealing but actually reducing the immoral tendencies of society, may be more accurately determined if we bear in mind a significant revelation from the report of the Board of State Charities of Massachusetts for the year 1875.

" In 1865, the whole number of persons in " all our prisons during the year did not much

But
Massachusetts
shows a
marked
increase of
immorality.

"exceed 10,000, and of these only 481 were in "the State Prison.   In 1875, the whole number "has exceeded 20,000, and the whole number in "the State Prison has been 852.

"Thus we see that detected crimes and misde- "meanors have doubled since the close of the "civil war ; while undetected and unpunished "crimes have increased at least as fast, and now "we find that there is hardly a State in the Union "or a country in the civilized world where atro- "cious and flagrant crime is so common as in "Massachusetts.

In ten
years ;.
Increase
in
population
23 per cent.;
increase in
crime 128
per cent. !

"With an increase of 23 per cent. in popu- "lation, the prison returns show an increase of "128 per cent. in crime!" *

The reform
that is
needed.

While we need not become fanatical on the subject of the "Bible in schools," at least until the sacred volume is more universally read and pondered at home, nor on that of "God in the. "Constitution," while God in the private and daily affairs of the citizen is so frequently and unscrupulously ignored ; still the practical and

---

* See Note III.

urgent need must sooner or later appear of a definite moral training for the youth of our nation, based upon something more than a whimsical patching up by the politic schoolmaster of maxims here and there, now of " honesty as the best policy," now of " all for "number one," now of " might makes right," or the survival of the fittest, now of " evil as un-" developed good," now of the " wickedness of " the world and the flesh," and now of " all for " the greater glory of God."

Has not the world been searching for this law that shall be to man's moral nature what the laws of thought are to his intellectual nature,—a law which shall determine absolutely the good and the evil, and tell him what to shun and what to exercise in training himself into harmony with the order of the universe? And if it has been reserved for this new age in which we live to arrive at this principle *of use* or mutual services as the primary law of the kingdom of God and all or-

Need of a definite moral aim and discipline.

derly society among men, while we may miss
the majestic outline of some vision of our fancy
in this plain and realistic principle, may we not
be thankful that we have so simple and practical an ethics as this to teach and impress upon
the youth of our age and to subject to the test
of experience? Use is the end itself to which
other motives, those of duty or self-control or
self-abnegation, yea, even the sacred exercises
of piety and religion, regarded as outward ordi-
nances and rites, all serve as means. The goal
is here at last reached and all the moral philosophy of the centuries finds its solution in this

The simplicity of the law of use: its practical character.

very simple and homely commonplace, that to
be good and to do good is to be useful.

Objections answered.

Is it objected that in making this the motive
of life, religion is ignored? I would protest
rather that rightly understood this is the sum
of religion, in that, to quote again the

Swedenborg's definition of religion.

language of Swedenborg,—" All religion has
" relation to life, and the life of religion is to
" do good."

And if it be objected, on the other hand, that all distinctions between religion and morality are henceforth blotted out, I would say that the world is so much the better off in being disabused of the delusion that morality, in the sense of doing right from purely selfish motives rather than from the principle of obedience to a Divine law of right and wrong, can confirm the good, or abolish the evil of the world; for no more than the devil can cast out devils, can the principle of self-love, impelled by its own motive only, cast out or mitigate in any degree the evils which it has brought into the world. *Morals and religion united.*

Not mere self-abnegation for its own sake, not the crushing out of instinct, and the mortifying of our natural faculties, but the subordination of the whole man to this one holy principle of use,—this will harmonize our life, and bring health, beauty, and joy again into the world in the very name of those once dreaded powers— morality and religion. Let our children be taught this principle from their earliest age; *Use the law of personal self-discipline.*

let parents inculcate it, schools teach it, and society exemplify it, and how much of our aimless, distracted moralizing and even legislating will soon vanish among the discarded errors of the past. Let it with children be made Children to a thing of absolute requirement, that they be be trained to be trained to be useful; let the idea of service useful. enter into every relation possible, at home, at school, and in the state. Let the much-abused term, " the dignity of labor," which is rapidly undergoing an evolution into the right of the laboring classes to be supported without labor, —let this give way to the *sacredness of service*, a sacredness derived from no lower source than the Divine Man Himself, who came to men " not to be ministered unto, but to minister."

And here I must say a word further in the *Use* not definition of use, lest I should be so unfortunate mere " utility " as to seem to inculcate a mere utility, or service of bodily and worldly interests, and to ignore the culture and exercise of the finer and higher faculties of our nature. While it is true that

no sense or taste exists in human nature so
highly refined as not to have some practical
use as its end, whether it be in the fine arts, in
literature, in religion, in the love of nature, or
of philosophy, it is equally true that the uses
which our faculties subserve, are of various
grades. There are affections to be delighted, Variety and multiplicity of uses.
and thoughts to be inspired, and impulses to
be stirred and strengthened, as well as bodies
to be clothed and fed in the world ; and how
large a part of the substantial good of human
life comes from these higher fields of service,
where the poet, the musician, the painter, the Uses of the fine arts.
skilful designer and decorator of our every-
day utensils, the architect, the orator, the his-
torian, and the philosopher, have cast in their
noble intellectual earnings into the wealth of
the ages ! Who shall calculate the stores of
delight contributed to humanity through end-
less generations by a single beautiful creation
of genius, by a single noble, helpful act of genuine charity, however humble and unpretend-

ing. Men live from delights, either good or

The *life* of
man to be
served. bad, and to contribute to the good delights in
those planes of· life which are higher than the
body, this is as truly of practical use to the
world as the clearing of forests, the plowing of
fields, and the weaving of fabrics.

So, too, the uses of life multiply almost infinitely when their complex and more general
forms are subject to the analysis of a true spiritual physiology. Man is a little world in himself,
and the human body is a picture in miniature,
not only of all the universe of mind within, but
of the universe of matter without, and not a
muscle or vein or cell or fibre in the human
body but corresponds in a mysterious and a
wonderful manner to some organ or faculty of
the mind ; so that the study of the mutual relation of all these minute particles and forms of
the human body, in the uses of the animal
economy, will enable us to judge by analogy of
the intricate and beautiful system in which
every emotion and intellectual activity of the

human mind may play its part in the kingdom
of social uses or in the collective man.

Let men cultivate, then, a *conscience of use ;*
so that the strong and healthy current of social
life shall be a steady sphere of happy labor,—
the doing, the achieving of something, and not
the idle and selfish consumption of the earnings
of others.* Let happiness be sought in useful
work, be it manual or mental, in the use adapted
to each, in his proper sphere or station. Let
the evils of mere intellectual culture, so often
stimulating to pride and mischievous cunning,
be made to give way, in proper measure, to industrial and artistic training, so that children may
learn at an early age the heavenly delight that
flows in only to the mind of him who works
unselfishly to add something to the treasure, the
good, the happiness of the world ; and let vices
be judged as vices, because they destroy usefulness, because they violate the Divine command :
"To love God with all our strength, and our
"neighbor as our self."

The conscience of use.

Industrial training.

Vices are whatever things are hurtful to use.

* See Note IV.

Will there be any difficulty in inculcating a
Catholicity of this doctrine. moral, nay, a religious system, such as this, in
the schools even of our free and tolerant repub-
lic?   Where is the sect or the party that can
raise a whisper of reproach against this holy
gospel of use, of mutual service of man to man,
as the very will and law of God?

We live in a strange age, an age of contra-
Anomalies of the present time, in morals and education. dictions, indeed ; an age which presents the
unprecedented spectacle of municipal and State
legislatures, on the same page of the statute-
The " law " banishes the Bible and sanctifies the Sabbath ! book, forbidding the use of the Bible in schools,
and enacting laws for keeping holy the Sab-
bath ; an age which thinks by legislation not
only to restrain man from crime by punishment,
but by prohibition of outward indulgence to
make him inwardly virtuous.   Is there not here
a confusion of police and educators?   If, indeed,
the temptation to vice comes only from without,
Temptations come from within : man needs reforming, not his surroundings. then may a heavenly state of society be within
the possibilities of any legislature of reformers;
but if, on the contrary, the temptations to vice

come not from without, but from within, if the man, and not his surroundings, need reforming, must we not begin in giving man a moral police within, a guardian stronger, more watchful, and more effectual than any outward agencies our legislatures can operate?

And is this inward police any thing else than conscience, and without this what is any reform, any prohibition of vice, but a mere whitening of the surface of that which remains foul and corrupt within, ready always to pour forth again when the restraint is removed? And where shall we begin in cultivating and educating this best guardian of society, the human conscience? I answer in that which is the beginning and ending of ethical and religious culture, for, so far as either is genuine and not a sham, they both constitute a one,—in this teaching our youth to know the law of mutual service as the Divinely imposed law of the highest happiness and highest good of man, to reverence it as the very soul of Divinity, to love it, to live by it.

Inefficiency of legislation in moral reforms.

How this principle is to be inculcated, I do
not regard it as necessary to discuss in further
detail here.   A useful life is the standard, the

The work
of ethical
education. aim, the pattern; the human will, with its emotions and desires, its likes and dislikes, is the
subject to be trained to conformity with this
standard, to attain to this good as an end; the
means is in the knowledge of the right or the
lawful as the useful, and of the wrong and un-
lawful as that which injures or destroys use;
and the implanting of this knowledge in the
mind and, by constant exercise, in the affections
of youth, and thus making it the law of life, is
the work of the ethical educator.

Let those who undertake this education re-

Ethics is a
practice not
an opinion. member, however, that the end is a moral, that
is, an affectional, and not an intellectual one;
that it is a practice and not an opinion that is
to be inculcated; and that while legislatures and

The force
to be used
a moral
one: which
leads but
does not
compel. governments may outwardly compel, educators
never may.   It is the swine-herd who drives his
flock; the shepherd leads his.

NOTE I.

THE author, while treating of his subject in a new form, desires to lay no claim to originality in the principles here presented, but rather to refer his readers to the more full elucidation of them to be found in the writings of Emanuel Swedenborg, especially in a posthumous work of this remarkable writer, entitled *De Divino Amore*, being a treatise attached to a larger work, *Apocalypsis Explicata.* To indicate the comprehensiveness of this doctrine of use as a Divinely established basis of ethics, it is only necessary to quote here the chapter headings of this treatise, which are in substance as follows :

That life, which is the Divine Love, is in a form.

That that form is a form of use.

That man, both in particular and in general, is in such a form.

That heaven is in such a form.

That all things of the world also tend to a similar form.

That there are as many uses as there are affections.

That there are genera and species of affections, and differences of species, in infinitum, and, in like manner, of uses.

That there are degrees of affections and uses.

That every use derives its life from the common use, and that from it flow in the necessary, the useful, and the delightful things of life, according to the quality of the use and the quality of its affection.

That so far as a man is in the love of use, so far he is in the love of the Lord, so far he loves Him, and loves his neighbor, and is a man.

That a man is not of sound mind unless use be his affection or occupation.

That a man has eternal life according to his affection of use.

That a man's will is his affection.

That, in the Word, to love means to perform uses. See John, xvi: 21, 24; xv: 9, 10; xxi: 15–17.

Etc., etc.

NOTE II.

IT is but just to recognize the distinction which exists between what may be called the egoistic and the altruistic schools of utilitarian moralists; but leaving aside the pure and avowed egoists, the followers of Helvetius, for instance, who declared self-love to be the foundation of all morals and all society, we are equally required to distinguish between two kinds of altruism, namely, between that which inculcates the love of others for the sake of others, and that inculcating the love of others for the sake of self. While the latter is, without doubt, only egoism or self-love, more or less effectually concealed, even from the subject himself, under the more amiable traits of charity or benevolence or public spirit, it is nevertheless available for the good of society in that Divine economy which regards the moral freedom of man as a most essential agent to his regeneration, and includes in its wise providence even the permission of evil. The element of selfishness, lurking more or less conspicuously in all human motives, must not lead us to utter self-condemnation. At the same time, the ideal to be striven for, and the standard of our real moral perfection, will remain the principle of a genuine altruism, namely, the love of others purely for their good, or, at least, the finding our own happiness first and chiefly in that of others. That this ultimately results in the highest happiness to one's self, does not detract from its purely altruistic character. Otherwise the perfection of society would be the negation of happiness. Our highest conception of the happiness of God must indeed be of that which He experiences in the happiness of His creatures, and this infinitely, yet without self-love.

NOTE III.

In citing the Massachusetts report, the author would not be understood as presuming to infer a law from a single example ; nevertheless, in all reasoning like this upon the method of " concomitant variations," it is of the first importance that all phases of a question be examined ; and the relation of intellectual education to crime manifestly embraces more than a mere comparison between the illiterate and the school-trained populace. The progress or the decline in morality of society as trained in our present public schools, is a more pertinent subject of inquiry. On this point, Mr. Richard Grant White has written some searching words in an article in the *North American Review* for December, 1880, entitled " The Public-School Failure." In this article further statistics from New England reports are given, which throw valuable light on the question of public morality as affecte/ by our own much-boasted free-school system.

NOTE IV.

In using this term, the *conscience of use*, the auth r would recall to the reader the analogy drawn in the earlier part of the essay between the physical, intellectual, and moral training. As one, by a kind of acquired intuition, recognizes that which is agreeable or revolting to the physical state, and so may be said to have always on

the alert a *conscience of the agreeable and the disagreeable,*
which governs his bodily actions ; and as, in like manner,
our *conscience of truth* is a constantly present standard,
by which we instinctively decide the verity or falsity of
statements, so the *conscience of use* is regarded as an acquired sense of being in harmony or in discord with the
objective good of the universe, a sense so quick and urgent that we are prompted rather by a persistent feeling
than by any reflection or reason to set ourselves right
with the Divine order of uses, in which our true happiness finally lies. This feeling can be described, perhaps,
as that satisfaction which is experienced in the pursuit of
all useful, congenial labor, or, in other words, in that labor
which is the particular use for which one is by his nature
fitted, and also that miserable unrest and sense of dis-
satisfaction which to all well-trained moral natures a
state of enforced idleness invariably produces. A stronger
than any magnetic current seems to drive and pulsate
through the whole moral universe, beating at the sources
of our life and calling us to work. If we yield and are
borne along, it becomes a stream of quiet, profound delight and peace. If we resist, or grow insensible, or lose
our *conscience of use,* we then become like the blind or
the deaf, to whom the beauty and the harmony of the
universe appeal in vain. The delight in pleasure is only
genuine delight when the pleasures are true *recreations,*

that is, when they restore the bodily and mental energies
for the renewal of those labors in which true happiness
dwells.

> " Rest is not quitting
>   The busy career ;
>   It is but the fitting
>   Of man to his sphere."

There is nothing unreasonable in teaching children to
regard their hours of study or busy occupation as their
essentially happiest ones, for such they undoubtedly are
when not accompanied with undue fatigue or excessive
confinement, and to look upon their pleasures as only
secondarily happy or as *instrumental* to the genuine happiness of work.   How strong the natural impulse to use
is, is beautifully shown in the peculiar delight a child
feels in those plays in which he believes himself to be
constructing or performing something of use, and his
manifest grief in finding that he was deceived when his
little creation is thoughtlessly cast aside by his parents.
And in the more mature experience of life, the happiness
of an employment is unquestionably enhanced by the
consciousness, even though it be a mistaken one, of its
usefulness ; while, on the other hand, the pleasures of leis-
ure, rest, and recreation are doubtless proportionate to
the sense of their having been fairly earned by useful in-

dustry, and of their contributing to our greater capacity for usefulness in the future.

And if the Divine Parent is more tenderly considerate than earthly ones in not so hastily dispelling the fond illusions of those of His children who are happy in the consciousness of useful endeavors, even though the result be one of mistaken importance to the great mass, still this will not be discordant with our conceptions of His love and of His perfect wisdom in the moral government of the world.

URBANA UNIVERSITY, O., *September*, 1881.

LIBRARY OF THE UNIVERSITY OF CALIFORNIA

www.ingramcontent.com/pod-product-compliance
Lightning Source LLC
Chambersburg PA
CBHW021531090426
42739CB00007B/884

*9 7 8 3 3 3 7 2 3 2 5 7 3 *